YUMA COUNTY LIBRARY DISTRICT

YUMA COUNTY
LIBRARY DISTRICT
2951 S. 21st Dr. Yuma, AZ 85364
(928) 782-1871
www.yumalibrary.org

Polar Vortex and Climate Change

A MODERN PERSPECTIVES BOOK

Tamra B. Orr

CHERRY LAKE
Publishing

Published in the United States of America by Cherry Lake Publishing
Ann Arbor, Michigan
www.cherrylakepublishing.com

Content Adviser: Satta Sarmah Hightower, Writer & Editor, Talented Tenth Media, Boston, MA
Reading Adviser: Marla Conn MS, Ed., Literacy specialist, Read-Ability, Inc.

Photo Credits: © CO Leong / Shutterstock.com, cover, 1; © arek_malang / Shutterstock.com, 4; © NicolasMcComber / iStock.com, 5; © nicolamargaret / iStock.com, 7; © VichoT / iStock.com, 9;© Designua / Shutterstock.com, 10;© Luiz Ferreira / Shutterstock.com, 11; © eddtoro / Shutterstock. com, 12, 15; Photographed by William O. Field on Aug. 13, 1941 (left) and by Bruce F. Molnia on Aug. 31, 2004 (right) / From the Glacier Photograph Collection / Boulder, Colorado USA: National Snow and Ice Data Center / World Data Center for Glaciology, 13; © Torgado / Shutterstock.com, 14; © Lightspring / Shutterstock.com, 17; © psdphotography / iStock.com, 19; © Susan Law Cain / Shutterstock.com, 20; © Amanda Sutcliffe / Shutterstock.com, 22; © milehightraveler / iStock.com, 23; © meliusphotography / iStock.com, 25; © dan_prat / iStock.com, 27; © GreenStockCreative / Shutterstock.com, 29; © FashionStock.com / Shutterstock.com, 30

Graphic Element Credits: ©RoyStudioEU/Shutterstock.com, back cover, front cover, multiple interior pages; ©queezz/Shutterstock.com, back cover, front cover, multiple interior pages

Library of Congress Cataloging-in-Publication Data
Names: Orr, Tamra B., author.
Title: Polar vortex and climate change / Tamra B. Orr.
Description: Ann Arbor : Cherry Lake Publishing, 2017. | Series: Modern perspectives
    | Includes bibliographical references and index.
Identifiers: LCCN 2016058627| ISBN 9781634728621 (hardcover) | ISBN 9781534100404
    (paperback) | ISBN 9781634729512 (PDF) | ISBN 9781534101296 (hosted ebook)
Subjects: LCSH: Polar vortex—Juvenile literature. | Climatic changes—Juvenile literature.
    | Winter—History—21st century—Juvenile literature.
Classification: LCC QC994.75 .O77 2017 | DDC 551.50911/3—dc23
LC record available at https://lccn.loc.gov/2016058627

Cherry Lake Publishing would like to acknowledge the work of
The Partnership for 21st Century Skills. Please visit *www.p21.org*
for more information.

Printed in the United States of America
Corporate Graphics

Table of Contents

In this book, you will read three different perspectives about the polar vortex, which occurred in early 2014. While these characters are fictionalized, each perspective is based on real things that happened to real people during and after the harsh weather. As you'll see, the same event can look different depending on one's point of view.

Chapter 1

Julianna Parker

College Student

"**I** just cannot understand this!" I said, slamming my hands down on the keyboard. I stared at the charts on the computer screen in front of me. How in the world people could look at evidence like this and then question if global **climate change** was real or not was beyond me. I had been studying weather patterns and data for the last 2 years, and I was completely convinced that Earth was heading for serious trouble.

"What now, Juli?" my friend Gabriel asked. He was used to my ranting and raving, since he had been my lab partner all year long. He usually focused on global temperatures, while I specialized in studying **glaciers**, Arctic waters, and worldwide sea levels.

▲ *Scientists understand the ways pollution and climate change are linked.*

"Did you see this latest report on Glacier National Park?" I asked, pointing at my monitor. "In 1910, it had more than 150 glaciers in it. Today, it has less than 30!" Gabe shook his head. "The newest prediction is that by the end of this century, the global sea levels may rise as high as another 6½ feet (2 meters). You know what that means?"

"Of course I do," Gabe replied. "Islands will be underwater, and so will lots of beaches and big cities—like New York."

"Don't people understand what is happening?" I asked. As temperatures went up, glaciers melted faster and water levels rose, and that caused flooding and much worse.

Second Source

▶ Find a second source that provides details about what is happening at Glacier National Park. Compare the information you find there to the information in this book.

▲ *Glaciers are dense bodies of ice that are constantly moving under their own weight.*

Think About It

▶ Reread this chapter. What is the main point Gabe is trying to make? What detail supports your answer?

Before I came to college, I had heard the terms *global warming* and *climate change* in the news, but admittedly paid little attention to them. It wasn't until I took my first science class that a professor had grabbed my attention—and I found myself fascinated.

As I learned more about global warming, I was shocked to find that there were people who did not believe it was a real phenomenon. Professor Cooper had told me that 97 percent of all climate scientists firmly believed climate-warming trends were happening. However, in a recent **poll**, a full one-quarter of Americans disagreed, and many of them regarded the entire issue as a **hoax**! Whenever I thought about that, I could feel myself getting angry—and confused. How could people see all the evidence and just deny it as accurate?

▲ *Much of the research on climate change is being done by scientists in Antarctica.*

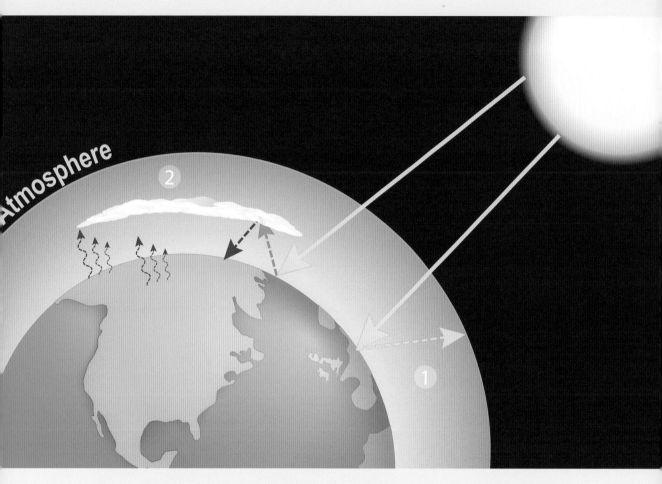

▲ *This image shows how heat from the sun travels both without greenhouse gases (1) and with greenhouse gases (2) in the atmosphere.*

"The planet is warming up," Gabe agreed. "Those **greenhouse gases** collect in our atmosphere like a thick blanket, and they trap the sun's heat. Unfortunately, people misunderstand how that affects the planet."

"I know," I said, shaking my head. "Like with this **polar vortex** they are predicting is going to hit the Midwest and East Coast any day now. Everyone asks, how can the world be getting hotter if we have these frigid temperatures?" I sighed. I wish I knew a way to reach out and explain the connection between warmer temperatures and colder winters, but I didn't know how to begin. Maybe by the time I

▲ *Drought is only one effect of climate change.*

▲ *Calling climate change global warming can be confusing.*

graduated in 2 years, more people would recognize what was happening to the planet. I just hoped Earth would hang in there while people caught up!

Changes Over Time

now you see it   now you don't

photo: William O. Field

photo: Bruce F. Molnia

Muir Glacier, Alaska: August 13, 1941 and August 31, 2004

NASA CLIMATE 365

climate365.tumblr.com | go.nasa.gov/climate365

Chapter 2

Jackson Miller
New York Student

I pulled on my slippers and yanked my hoodie a little tighter. I knew the thermostat said it was 68 degrees Fahrenheit (20 degrees Celsius) in our house, but it didn't feel that warm. Part of the problem was hearing the wind whistling past the windows and seeing the snow piling up outside.

"Brrrrr," said my mom, coming into the living room to glance at the thermostat. "I just can't seem to keep warm tonight, Jackson. The whole world seems to be whining about global warming, but one glance out the window is enough to prove that's a silly theory."

My mom definitely didn't believe in the whole climate change concept. When I showed her some of the information I had learned

▲ *Many states across the country hit record low temperatures in January 2014.*

in school, she always answered me the same way. "Temperatures have gone up and down in cycles forever, and this is nothing new. Don't worry about it."

I turned on the television to catch the latest weather report. School had already been canceled for tomorrow, so I was hoping the polar vortex would last a few days longer. "Folks, it's time to stay inside, heat up some hot chocolate, and catch up on your reading," the reporter stated. "Our temperatures are going to be 25 to 30 degrees colder than usual, and we will definitely go below zero before this is all over."

"What is a polar vortex anyway?" I asked Mom. As if he had heard me, the reporter said, "For those of you who aren't sure what a polar vortex is, let me explain."

 ## Second Source

▶ Find a second source that addresses the issue of temperatures going up and down over time. How does the information there compare to the information in this book?

Pointing to a photo of the earth, he continued, "The extremely cold pocket of air over the North Pole or Arctic region is called the polar vortex. It's always there and, by itself, is not a problem. Usually this cold air just keeps swirling in a circle from west to east, kept in place by the planet's **jet stream**."

Mom curled up on the couch, and I sat down next to her.

▲ *The polar vortex always exists over the North Pole.*

Analyze This

▶ How does Jackson's perspective appear to differ from his mother's? How are they similar?

"If that polar vortex weakens at all, it begins to spread out and patches of cold air start creeping down the planet," the newscaster added. "Then we are hit with below zero temperatures. If the air has moisture in it, we also get lots of snow—like we're getting right now."

"That makes sense," Mom said. "But I wonder what makes the polar vortex weaken in the first place."

"Most experts believe a weakened polar vortex is caused by global warming," the news reporter stated. Mom rolled her eyes, but I listened carefully.

"As temperatures rise, glaciers melt. The Arctic sea levels go up, and the water gets warmer. This extra water **evaporates** into the atmosphere, and that weakens the polar vortex. In other words, global warming means colder, harsher winters."

▲ *Giant chunks of ice break off from glaciers as they melt.*

▲ *In 2014, 122 inches (310 centimeters) of snow fell in Buffalo, New York.*

Interesting, I thought. I knew Mom still didn't agree, but just in case, I was going to add some socks under these slippers. It wasn't going to warm up anytime soon!

Swinging Temperatures

	Chicago, IL	Dallas, TX	Indianapolis, IN	Washington, DC	New York, NY
Average High/Low Temperatures	32/19	56/37	35/21	43/29	38/27
Jan. 5, 2014	31/-1	60/22	35/5	42/31	40/27
Jan. 6, 2014	-1/-15	33/14	5/-15	49/11	55/19
Jan. 7, 2014	5/-11	47/22	8/-14	21/6	19/4
Jan. 8, 2014	15/-2	49/38	25/6	31/13	22/9

Temperatures are provided in degrees Fahrenheit.

Chapter 3

Christopher Williams

Coal Miner

I tried to keep my focus on work, but it was hard. The boss's speech this morning had upset me, and I was finding it difficult to not dwell on his dire predictions about our jobs.

"The East Coast is getting hammered by some pretty rough winter weather," Mr. Hernandez had said. "This polar vortex, as they're calling it, is being blamed on global warming."

"Like everything else, right Chris?" my friend Louie mumbled.

"Every time people bring up climate change," the boss continued, "you know they're eventually going to complain about burning **fossil fuels**. And that means more rules and regulations and more

▲ *Most cars run on gasoline or diesel—these are both fossil fuels.*

Think About It

▶ Why would people automatically associate coal miners with global warming? Give two reasons to support your answer.

pressure on us. It means our jobs are always in **jeopardy** when these topics make headlines." He sighed deeply and then said, "All right, men. Nothing to do about this today, so back to work! Be quick, be smart, and be careful!"

I ran through the pouring rain and back into the mine. One thing you could say about being a miner: You didn't have to deal with lousy weather. I went down to the bottom of the mine, and, as usual, I was astonished at how dark it was this far below the ground. It took a special type of person to cope with being a coal miner. I'm 40 years old and had been doing it since I was 20, and the darkness had become like a friend to me.

Coal mining had come a long way over the years. The days of picks and shovels were largely over. Now everything is **automated**.

▲ *In 2015, mining was listed as the sixth most dangerous job in the United States.*

Clean Coal?

According to Greenpeace International, an environmental organization, "Coal is the single greatest threat to our climate," due to the emissions and gases it creates when burned for heat and energy. In addition to contributing to global warming, the group also says coal mining increases the world's water crisis, pollutes the air, and destroys forests. Despite this, coal has been the main energy source for the world since 2003.

Heavy machines and huge vehicles are used daily. I work with the continuous miner, a machine that digs the tunnels by remote control. It weighs more than 50 tons! It has a conveyor belt on it that's more than 3 feet (1 m) wide, and I can load 12 tons of coal in under a minute if the day is going well.

▲ *Coal accounts for about 33 percent of energy used in the United States.*

Second Source

▶ Find a second source that explains what coal is used for in the United States. How does the information from that source compare to the information in this book?

I actually really love my job. I am good at it, and I like going home knowing that my hard work will result in people having heat and electricity.

Of course, I worried about global warming. Who didn't? I had heard about the cold weather hitting the East Coast and felt sorry for everyone who had to cope with it. I had read about sea ice melting and temperatures rising, and I did what I could from home. I had replaced all of our incandescent lightbulbs with fluorescents. I kept the thermostat down two degrees in the winter and up two degrees in the summer. I replaced the furnace filter on a regular basis.

My job as a coal miner is important, and I am proud of what I do. I will keep doing it and keep putting food on my family's table. I just hoped the East Coast would warm up soon, so the headlines would change!

▲ *Making small changes around your home can help you consume less energy.*

Look, Look Again

This photo shows city streets in Brooklyn, New York, in January 2014. Use it to help you answer the following questions:

1. How would a climate scientist describe this photo to friends? What would she say when asked about global warming?

2. How would a family who lived in Brooklyn feel about this photo? How might they describe the weather in 2014?

3. What concerns might someone who worked in the coal industry have when seeing this picture?

Glossary

automated (AW-tuh-mayt-id) made to operate automatically by using machines

climate change (KLYE-mit CHAYNJ) global warming and other changes in the weather and weather patterns that are happening because of human activity

evaporates (ih-VAP-uh-rates) changes from a liquid to a vapor or gas

fossil fuels (FAH-suhl FYOOLZ) coal, oil, or natural gas, formed from the remains of prehistoric plants and animals

glaciers (GLAY-shurz) large ice masses

greenhouse gases (GREEN-hous GAS-iz) gases like carbon dioxide, methane, and ozone

hoax (HOHKS) an act intended to trick people into believing something is real when it is not

jeopardy (JEP-ur-dee) danger of loss, harm, or failure

jet stream (JET STREEM) a very strong current of wind, usually found between 6 and 9 miles (10 and 14.5 kilometers) above the earth's surface, moving west to east

polar vortex (POH-lur VOR-teks) strong stream of extremely cold air that is stationed above the North Pole

poll (POHL) survey of the public

Learn More

Further Reading

Danks, Fiona, and Jo Schofield. *The Wild Weather Book*. London: Frances Lincoln, 2013.

Griffin, Mary. *Earth's Coldest Places*. New York: Gareth Stevens, 2015.

Hoena, Blake. *If It's Really Cold . . . and Other Weather Predictions*. North Mankato, MN: Capstone Press, 2012.

Mooney, Carla. *Surviving in Cold Places*. Minneapolis: Lerner Publications Company, 2014.

Yomtov, Nel. *The Children's Blizzard of 1888: A Cause-and-Effect Investigation*. Minneapolis: Lerner Publications, 2017.

Web Sites

EPA—A Student's Guide to Global Climate Change
https://www3.epa.gov/climatechange/kids

NASA—Climate Kids: What Is "Global Climate Change"?
http://climatekids.nasa.gov/climate-change-meaning

Time for Kids—The Polar Vortex
www.timeforkids.com/news/polar-vortex/136731

Index

About the Author

Tamra Orr remembers watching the news reports about the frigid weather in the East. She was especially grateful she lived on the opposite coast. She is the author of hundreds of books for readers of all ages. She lives in the Pacific Northwest with her family and spends all of her free time writing letters, reading books, and going camping. She graduated from Ball State University with a degree in English and education and believes she has the best job in the world. It gives her the chance to keep learning all about the world and the people in it.